30 Short Surahs for Beginners

Contents

Surah Al Fatiha

1. Bismillaahir Rahmaanir Raheem
2. Alhamdu lillaahi Rabbil 'aalameen
3. Ar-Rahmaanir-Raheem
4. Maaliki Yawmid-Deen
5. Iyyaaka na'budu wa Iyyaaka nasta'een
6. Ihdinas-Siraatal-Mustaqeem
7. Siraatal-lazeena an'amta 'alaihim ghayril-maghdoobi 'alaihim wa lad-daaalleen

1. In the name of Allah, Most Gracious, Most Merciful.
2. Praise be to Allah, the Cherisher and Sustainer of the worlds;
3. Most Gracious, Most Merciful;
4. Master of the Day of Judgment.
5. Thee do we worship, and Thine aid we seek.
6. Show us the straight way,
7. The way of those on whom Thou hast bestowed Thy Grace, those whose (portion) is not wrath, and who go not astray.

Surah At-Takathu

Bismillaahir Rahmaanir Raheem

1. Al haaku mut takathur
2. Hatta zurtumul-maqaabir
3. Kalla sawfa ta'lamoon
4. Thumma kalla sawfa ta'lamoon
5. Kalla law ta'lamoona 'ilmal yaqeen
6. Latara-wun nal jaheem
7. Thumma latara wunnaha 'ainal yaqeen
8. Thumma latus alunna yauma-izin 'anin na'eem

In the name of Allah, Most Gracious, Most Merciful.

1. The mutual rivalry for piling up (the good things of this world) diverts you (from the more serious things),
2. Until ye visit the graves.
3. But nay, ye soon shall know (the reality).
4. Again, ye soon shall know!
5. Nay, were ye to know with certainty of mind, (ye would beware!)
6. Ye shall certainly see Hell-Fire!
7. Again, ye shall see it with certainty of sight!
8. Then, shall ye be questioned that Day about the joy (ye indulged in!).

Surah Al-Qari'ah

Bismillaahir Rahmaanir Raheem

1. Al qaari'ah
2. Mal qaariah
3. Wa maa adraaka mal qaari'ah
4. Yauma ya koonun naasu kal farashil mabthooth
5. Wa ta koonul jibalu kal 'ihnil manfoosh
6. Fa-amma man thaqulat mawa zeenuh
7. Fahuwa fee 'ishatir raadiyah
8. Wa amma man khaffat mawa zeenuh
9. Fa-ummuhu haawiyah
10. Wa maa adraaka maa hiyah
11. Naarun hamiyah

In the name of Allah, Most Gracious, Most Merciful.

1. The (Day) of Noise and Clamour:
2. What is the (Day) of Noise and Clamour?
3. And what will explain to thee what the (Day) of Noise and Clamour is?
4. (It is) a Day whereon men will be like moths scattered about,
5. And the mountains will be like carded wool.
6. Then, he whose balance (of good deeds) will be (found) heavy,
7. Will be in a life of good pleasure and satisfaction.
8. But he whose balance (of good deeds) will be (found) light,-
9. Will have his home in a (bottomless) Pit.
10. And what will explain to thee what this is?
11. (It is) a Fire Blazing fiercely!

Surah Al-Asr

Bismillaahir Rahmaanir Raheem

1. Wal' asr
2. Innal insaana lafee khusr
3. Il lal lazeena aamanu wa 'amilus saali haati wa tawa saw bil haqqi wa tawa saw bis sabr

In the name of Allah, Most Gracious, Most Merciful.

1. By (the Token of) Time (through the ages),
2. Verily Man is in loss,
3. Except such as have Faith, and do righteous deeds, and (join together) in the mutual teaching of Truth, and of Patience and Constancy.

Surah Al-Humazah

Bismillaahir Rahmaanir Raheem

1. Wai lul-li kulli hu mazatil-lumaza
2. Al-lazi jama'a maalanw wa 'addadah
3. Yahsabu anna maalahooo akhladah
4. Kallaa; layunn ba zanna fil hutamah
5. Wa maa adraaka mal-hutamah
6. Narul laahil-mooqada
7. Al latee tat tali'u 'alal afidah
8. Innahaa 'alaihim mu' sada
9. Fee 'amadin mumad dadah

In the name of Allah, Most Gracious, Most Merciful.

1. Woe to every (kind of) scandal-monger and-backbiter,
2. Who pileth up wealth and layeth it by,
3. Thinking that his wealth would make him last for ever!
4. By no means! He will be sure to be thrown into That which Breaks to Pieces,
5. And what will explain to thee That which Breaks to Pieces?
6. (It is) the Fire of (the Wrath of) Allah kindled (to a blaze),
7. The which doth mount (Right) to the Hearts:
8. It shall be made into a vault over them,
9. In columns outstretched.

Surah Al-Fil

Bismillaahir Rahmaanir Raheem

1. Alam tara kaifa fa'ala rabbuka bi ashaabil feel
2. Alam yaj'al kai dahum fee tad leel
3. Wa arsala 'alaihim tairan abaabeel
4. Tar meehim bi hi jaaratim min sij jeel
5. Faja 'alahum ka'asfim m'akool

In the name of Allah, Most Gracious, Most Merciful.

1. Seest thou not how thy Lord dealt with the Companions of the Elephant?
2. Did He not make their treacherous plan go astray?
3. And He sent against them Flights of Birds,
4. Striking them with stones of baked clay.
5. Then did He make them like an empty field of stalks and straw, (of which the corn) has been eaten up.

Surah Quraish

Bismillaahir Rahmaanir Raheem

1. Li-ilaafi quraish
2. Elaafihim rihlatash shitaa-i wass saif
3. Fal y'abudu rabba haazal-bait
4. Allazi at'amahum min ju'inw-wa-aamana hum min khawf

In the name of Allah, Most Gracious, Most Merciful.

1. For the covenants (of security and safeguard enjoyed) by the Quraish,
2. Their covenants (covering) journeys by winter and summer,-
3. Let them adore the Lord of this House,
4. Who provides them with food against hunger, and with security against fear (of danger).

Surah Al-Maun

Bismillaahir Rahmaanir Raheem

1. Ara-aital lazee yu kazzibu bid deen
2. Fa zaalikal lazi yadu'ul-yateem
3. Wa la ya huddu 'alaa ta'amil miskeen
4. Fa wai lul-lil mu salleen
5. Al lazeena hum 'an salaatihim sahoon
6. Al lazeena hum yuraa-oon
7. Wa yamna'oonal ma'oon

In the name of Allah, Most Gracious, Most Merciful.

1. Seest thou one who denies the Judgment (to come)?
2. Then such is the (man) who repulses the orphan (with harshness),
3. And encourages not the feeding of the indigent.
4. So woe to the worshippers
5. Who are neglectful of their prayers,
6. Those who (want but) to be seen (of men),
7. But refuse (to supply) (even) neighbourly needs.

Surah Al-Kauthar

Bismillaahir Rahmaanir Raheem

1. Innaa a'taina kal kauthar
2. Fa salli li rabbika wanhar
3. Inna shani-aka huwal abtar

In the name of Allah, Most Gracious, Most Merciful.

1. To thee have we granted the Fount (of Abundance).
2. Therefore to thy Lord turn in Prayer and Sacrifice.
3. For he who hateth thee, he will be cut off (from Future Hope).

Surah Al-Kafirun

Bismillaahir Rahmaanir Raheem

1. Qul yaa-ai yuhal kaafiroon
2. Laa a'budu ma t'abudoon
3. Wa laa antum 'aabidoona maa a'bud
4. Wa laa ana 'abidum maa 'abattum
5. Wa laa antum 'aabidoona ma a'bud
6. Lakum deenukum wa liya deen.

In the name of Allah, Most Gracious, Most Merciful.

1. Say: O ye that reject Faith!
2. I worship not that which ye worship,
3. Nor will ye worship that which I worship.
4. And I will not worship that which ye have been wont to worship,
5. Nor will ye worship that which I worship.
6. To you be your Way, and to me mine.

Surah An-Nasr

Bismillaahir Rahmaanir Raheem

1. Iza jaa-a nas rullahi walfath
2. Wa ra-aitan naasa yadkhuloona fee deenil laahi afwajah
3. Fa sab bih bihamdi rabbika was taghfir, innahu kaana tawwaaba

In the name of Allah, Most Gracious, Most Merciful.

1. When comes the Help of Allah, and Victory,
2. And thou dost see the people enter Allah's Religion in crowds,
3. Celebrate the praises of thy Lord, and pray for His Forgiveness: For He is Oft-Returning (in Grace and Mercy).

Surah Al-Lahab

Bismillaahir Rahmaanir Raheem

1. Tab bat yadaa abee Lahabinw-wa tabb
2. Maa aghna 'anhu maaluhu wa ma kasab
3. Sa yas laa naran zaata lahab
4. Wam ra-atuhu hamma latal-hatab
5. Fee jeediha hab lum mim-masad

In the name of Allah, Most Gracious, Most Merciful.

1. Perish the hands of the Father of Flame! Perish he!
2. No profit to him from all his wealth, and all his gains!
3. Burnt soon will he be in a Fire of Blazing Flame!
4. His wife shall carry the (crackling) wood - As fuel!-
5. A twisted rope of palm-leaf fibre round her (own) neck!

Surah Al-Falaq
Bismillaahir Rahmaanir Raheem

1. Qul a'uzoo bi rabbil-falaq
2. Min sharri ma khalaq
3. Wa min sharri ghasiqin iza waqab
4. Wa min sharrin-naffaa-thaati fil 'uqad
5. Wa min sharri haasidin izaa hasad

In the name of Allah, Most Gracious, Most Merciful.

1. Say: I seek refuge with the Lord of the Dawn
2. From the mischief of created things;
3. From the mischief of Darkness as it overspreads;
4. From the mischief of those who practise secret arts;
5. And from the mischief of the envious one as he practises envy

Surah An-Nas

Bismillaahir Rahmaanir Raheem

1. Qul a'uzu birabbin naas
2. Malikin naas
3. Ilaahin naas
4. Min sharril was waasil khannaas
5. Al lazee yuwas wisu fee sudoorin naas
6. Minal jinnati wan naas

In the name of Allah, Most Gracious, Most Merciful.

1. Say: I seek refuge with the Lord and Cherisher of Mankind,
2. The King (or Ruler) of Mankind,
3. The god (or judge) of Mankind,-
4. From the mischief of the Whisperer (of Evil), who withdraws (after his whisper),-
5. (The same) who whispers into the hearts of Mankind,-
6. Among Jinns and among men.

Surah Al-Zilzal

Bismillaahir Rahmaanir Raheem

1. Izaa zul zilatil ardu zil zaalaha
2. Wa akh rajatil ardu athqaalaha
3. Wa qaalal insaanu ma laha
4. Yawmaa izin tuhad dithu akhbaaraha
5. Bi-anna rabbaka awhaa laha
6. Yawma iziny yas durun naasu ash tatal liyuraw a'maalahum
7. Famaiy ya'mal mithqala zarratin khai raiy-yarah
8. Wa maiy-y'amal mithqala zarratin sharraiy-yarah

In the name of Allah, Most Gracious, Most Merciful.

1. When the earth is shaken to her (utmost) convulsion,
2. And the earth throws up her burdens (from within),
3. And man cries (distressed): 'What is the matter with her?'-
4. On that Day will she declare her tidings:
5. For that thy Lord will have given her inspiration.
6. On that Day will men proceed in companies sorted out, to be shown the deeds that they (had done).
7. Then shall anyone who has done an atom's weight of good, see it!
8. And anyone who has done an atom's weight of evil, shall see it.

Surah Al-Adiyat

Bismillaahir Rahmaanir Raheem

1. Wal'aadi yaati dabha
2. Fal moori yaati qadha
3. Fal mugheeraati subha
4. Fa atharna bihee naq'a
5. Fawa satna bihee jam'a
6. Innal-insana lirabbihee lakanood
7. Wa innahu 'alaa zaalika la shaheed
8. Wa innahu lihubbil khairi la shadeed
9. Afala ya'lamu iza b'uthira ma filquboor
10. Wa hussila maa fis sudoor
11. Inna rabbahum bihim yauma 'izil la khabeer

In the name of Allah, Most Gracious, Most Merciful.

1. By the (Steeds) that run, with panting (breath),
2. And strike sparks of fire,
3. And push home the charge in the morning,
4. And raise the dust in clouds the while,
5. And penetrate forthwith into the midst (of the foe) en masse;-
6. Truly man is, to his Lord, ungrateful;
7. And to that (fact) he bears witness (by his deeds);
8. And violent is he in his love of wealth.
9. Does he not know,- when that which is in the graves is scattered abroad
10. And that which is (locked up) in (human) breasts is made manifest-
11. That their Lord had been Well-acquainted with them, (even to) that Day?

Surah Al-Bayyinah

Bismillaahir Rahmaanir Raheem

1. Lam ya kunil lazeena kafaru min ahlil kitaabi wal mushri keena mun fak keena hattaa ta-tiya humul bayyinah
2. Rasoolum minal laahi yatlu suhufam mutahharah
3. Feeha kutubun qaiyimah
4. Wa maa tafarraqal lazeena ootul kitaaba il-la mim b'adi ma jaa-at humul baiyyinah
5. Wa maa umiroo il-la liy'abu dul laaha mukhliseena lahud-deena huna faa-a wa yuqeemus salaata wa yu-tuz zakaata; wa zaalika deenul qaiyimah
6. Innal lazeena kafaru min ahlil kitaabi wal mushri keena fee nari jahan nama khaali deena feeha; ulaa-ika hum shar rul ba reeyah
7. Innal lazeena aamanu wa 'amilus saalihaati ula-ika hum khairul bareey yah
8. Jazaa-uhum inda rabbihim jan naatu 'adnin tajree min tahtihal an haaru khalideena feeha abada; radiy-yallaahu 'anhum wa ra du 'an zaalika liman khashiya rabbah.

In the name of Allah, Most Gracious, Most Merciful.

1. Those who reject (Truth), among the People of the Book and among the Polytheists, were not going to depart (from their ways) until there should come to them Clear Evidence,-
2. An messenger from Allah, rehearsing scriptures kept pure and holy:
3. Wherein are laws (or decrees) right and straight.
4. Nor did the People of the Book make schisms, until after there came to them Clear Evidence.
5. And they have been commanded no more than this: To worship Allah, offering Him sincere devotion, being true (in faith); to establish regular prayer; and to practise regular charity; and that is the Religion Right and Straight.

6. Those who reject (Truth), among the People of the Book and among the Polytheists, will be in Hell-Fire, to dwell therein (for aye). They are the worst of creatures.
7. Those who have faith and do righteous deeds,- they are the best of creatures.
8. Their reward is with Allah: Gardens of Eternity, beneath which rivers flow; they will dwell therein for ever; Allah well pleased with them, and they with Him: all this for such as fear their Lord and Cherisher.

Surah Al-Qadr

Bismillaahir Rahmaanir Raheem

1. Innaa anzalnaahu fee lailatil qadr
2. Wa maa adraaka ma lailatul qadr
3. Lailatul qadri khairum min alfee shahr
4. Tanaz zalul malaa-ikatu war roohu feeha bi izni-rab bihim min kulli amr
5. Salaamun hiya hattaa mat la'il fajr

In the name of Allah, Most Gracious, Most Merciful.

1. We have indeed revealed this (Message) in the Night of Power:
2. And what will explain to thee what the night of power is?
3. The Night of Power is better than a thousand months.
4. Therein come down the angels and the Spirit by Allah's permission, on every errand:
5. Peace! This until the rise of morn!

Surah Ad-Duha

Bismillaahir Rahmaanir Raheem

1. Wad duhaa
2. Wal laili iza sajaa
3. Ma wad da'aka rabbuka wa ma qalaa
4. Walal-aakhiratu khairul laka minal-oola
5. Wa la sawfa y'uteeka rabbuka fatarda
6. Alam ya jidka yateeman fa aawaa
7. Wa wa jadaka daal lan fahada
8. Wa wa jadaka 'aa-ilan fa aghnaa
9. Fa am mal yateema fala taqhar
10. Wa am mas saa-ila fala tanhar
11. Wa amma bi ni'mati rabbika fahad dith

In the name of Allah, Most Gracious, Most Merciful.

1. By the Glorious Morning Light,
2. And by the Night when it is still,-
3. Thy Guardian-Lord hath not forsaken thee, nor is He displeased.
4. And verily the Hereafter will be better for thee than the present.
5. And soon will thy Guardian-Lord give thee (that wherewith) thou shalt be well-pleased.
6. Did He not find thee an orphan and give thee shelter (and care)?
7. And He found thee wandering, and He gave thee guidance.
8. And He found thee in need, and made thee independent.
9. Therefore, treat not the orphan with harshness,
10. Nor repulse the petitioner (unheard);
11. But the bounty of the Lord - rehearse and proclaim!

Surah At-Tin

Bismillaahir Rahmaanir Raheem

1. Wat teeni waz zaitoon
2. Wa toori sineen
3. Wa haazal balad-il ameen
4. Laqad khalaqnal insaana fee ahsani taqweem
5. Thumma ra dad naahu asfala saafileen
6. Ill-lal lazeena aamanoo wa 'amilus saalihaati; falahum ajrun ghairu mamnoon
7. Fama yu kaz zibuka b'adu bid deen
8. Alai sal laahu bi-ahkamil haakimeen

In the name of Allah, Most Gracious, Most Merciful.

1. By the Fig and the Olive,
2. And the Mount of Sinai,
3. And this City of security,-
4. We have indeed created man in the best of moulds,
5. Then do We abase him (to be) the lowest of the low,-
6. Except such as believe and do righteous deeds: For they shall have a reward unfailing.
7. Then what can, after this, contradict thee, as to the judgment (to come)?
8. Is not Allah the wisest of judges?

Surah Al-Inshirah

Bismillaahir Rahmaanir Raheem

1. Alam nashrah laka sadrak
2. Wa wa d'ana 'anka wizrak
3. Allazee anqada zahrak
4. Wa raf 'ana laka zikrak
5. Fa inna ma'al usri yusra
6. Inna ma'al 'usri yusra
7. Fa iza faragh ta fansab
8. Wa ilaa rabbika far ghab

In the name of Allah, Most Gracious, Most Merciful.

1. Have We not expanded thee thy breast?-
2. And removed from thee thy burden
3. The which did gall thy back?-
4. And raised high the esteem (in which) thou (art held)?
5. So, verily, with every difficulty, there is relief:
6. Verily, with every difficulty there is relief.
7. Therefore, when thou art free (from thine immediate task), still labour hard,
8. And to thy Lord turn (all) thy attention.

Surah Ash-Shams

Bismillaahir Rahmaanir Raheem

1. Wash shamsi wa duhaa haa
2. Wal qamari izaa talaa haa
3. Wannahaari izaa jallaa haa
4. Wallaili izaa yaghshaa haa
5. Wassamaaa'i wa maa banaahaa
6. Wal ardi wa maa tahaahaa
7. Wa nafsinw wa maa sawwaahaa
8. Fa-alhamahaa fujoorahaa wa taqwaahaa
9. Qad aflaha man zakkaahaa
10. Wa qad khaaba man dassaahaa
11. Kazzabat Samoodu bi taghwaahaaa
12. Izim ba'asa ashqaahaa
13. Faqaala lahum Rasoolul laahi naaqatal laahi wa suqiyaahaa
14. Fakazzaboohu fa'aqaroohaa fadamdama 'alaihim Rabbuhum bizambihim fasaw waahaa
15. Wa laa yakhaafu'uqbaahaa

In the name of Allah, Most Gracious, Most Merciful.

1. By the Sun and his (glorious) splendour;
2. By the Moon as she follows him;
3. By the Day as it shows up (the Sun´s) glory;
4. By the Night as it conceals it;
5. By the Firmament and its (wonderful) structure;
6. By the Earth and its (wide) expanse:
7. By the Soul, and the proportion and order given to it;
8. And its enlightenment as to its wrong and its right;-
9. Truly he succeeds that purifies it,
10. And he fails that corrupts it!
11. The Thamud (people) rejected (their prophet) through their inordinate wrong-doing,
12. Behold, the most wicked man among them was deputed (for impiety).

13. But the Messenger of Allah said to them: "It is a She-camel of Allah! And (bar her not from) having her drink!"
14. Then they rejected him (as a false prophet), and they hamstrung her. So their Lord, on account of their crime, obliterated their traces and made them equal (in destruction, high and low)!
15. And for Him is no fear of its consequences.

Surah Al-Balad

Bismillaahir Rahmaanir Raheem

1. Laaa uqsimu bihaazal balad
2. Wa anta hillum bihaazal balad
3. Wa waalidinw wa maa walad
4. Laqad khalaqnal insaana fee kabad
5. Ayahsabu al-lai yaqdira 'alaihi ahad
6. Yaqoolu ahlaktu maalal lubadaa
7. Ayahsabu al lam yarahooo ahad
8. Alam naj'al lahoo 'aynayn
9. Wa lisaananw wa shafatayn
10. Wa hadaynaahun najdayn
11. Falaq tahamal-'aqabah
12. Wa maaa adraaka mal'aqabah
13. Fakku raqabah
14. Aw it'aamun fee yawmin zee masghabah
15. Yateeman zaa maqrabah
16. Aw miskeenan zaa matrabah
17. Summa kaana minal lazeena aamanoo wa tawaasaw bissabri wa tawaasaw bilmarhamah
18. Ulaaa'ika As-haabul maimanah
19. Wallazeena kafaroo bi aayaatinaa hum as-haabul Mash'amah
20. Alaihim naarum mu'sadah

In the name of Allah, Most Gracious, Most Merciful.

1. I do call to witness this City;-
2. And thou art a freeman of this City;-
3. And (the mystic ties of) parent and child;-
4. Verily We have created man into toil and struggle.
5. Thinketh he, that none hath power over him?
6. He may say (boastfully); Wealth have I squandered in abundance!
7. Thinketh he that none beholdeth him?
8. Have We not made for him a pair of eyes?-
9. And a tongue, and a pair of lips?-

48

10. And shown him the two highways?
11. But he hath made no haste on the path that is steep.
12. And what will explain to thee the path that is steep?-
13. (It is:) freeing the bondman;
14. Or the giving of food in a day of privation
15. To the orphan with claims of relationship,
16. Or to the indigent (down) in the dust.
17. Then will he be of those who believe, and enjoin patience, (constancy, and self-restraint), and enjoin deeds of kindness and compassion.
18. Such are the Companions of the Right Hand.
19. But those who reject Our Signs, they are the (unhappy) Companions of the Left Hand.
20. On them will be Fire vaulted over (all round).

Surah Al-Infitaar

Bismillaahir Rahmaanir Raheem

1. Izas samaaa'un fatarat
2. Wa izal kawaakibun tasarat
3. Wa izal bihaaru fujjirat
4. Wa izal qubooru bu'sirat
5. 'Alimat nafsum maa qaddamat wa akhkharat
6. Yaaa ayyuhal insaaanu maa gharraka bi Rabbikal kareem
7. Allazee khalaqaka fasaw waaka fa'adalak
8. Feee ayye sooratim maa shaaa'a rakkabak
9. Kalla bal tukazziboona bid deen
10. Wa inna 'alaikum lahaa fizeen
11. Kiraaman kaatibeen
12. Ya'lamoona ma taf'aloon
13. Innal abraara lafee na'eem
14. Wa innal fujjaara lafee jaheem
15. Yaslawnahaa Yawmad Deen
16. Wa maa hum 'anhaa bighaaa 'ibeen
17. Wa maaa adraaka maa Yawmud Deen
18. Summa maaa adraaka maa Yawmud Deen
19. Yawma laa tamliku nafsul linafsin shai'anw walamru yawma'izil lillaah

In the name of Allah, Most Gracious, Most Merciful.

1. When the Sky is cleft asunder;
2. When the Stars are scattered;
3. When the Oceans are suffered to burst forth;
4. And when the Graves are turned upside down;-
5. (Then) shall each soul know what it hath sent forward and (what it hath) kept back.
6. O man! What has seduced thee from thy Lord Most Beneficent?-
7. Him Who created thee. Fashioned thee in due proportion, and gave thee a just bias;
8. In whatever Form He wills, does He put thee together.
9. Nay! But ye do reject Right and Judgment!

10. But verily over you (are appointed angels) to protect you,-
11. Kind and honourable,- Writing down (your deeds):
12. They know (and understand) all that ye do.
13. As for the Righteous, they will be in bliss;
14. And the Wicked - they will be in the Fire,
15. Which they will enter on the Day of Judgment,
16. And they will not be able to keep away therefrom.
17. And what will explain to thee what the Day of Judgment is?
18. Again, what will explain to thee what the Day of Judgment is?
19. (It will be) the Day when no soul shall have power (to do) aught for another: For the command, that Day, will be (wholly) with Allah.

Surah Al-Jumua

Bismillaahir Rahmaanir Raheem

1. Yusabbihu lilaahi maa fis samaawaati wa maa fil ardil Malikil Quddoosil 'Azeezil Hakeem

2. Huwal lazee ba'asa fil ummiyyeena Rasoolam min hum yatloo 'alaihim aayaatihee wa yuzakkeehim wa yu'allimuhumul Kitaaba wal Hikmata wa in kaanoo min qablu lafee dalaalim mubeen

3. Wa aakhareena minhum lammaa yalhaqoo bihim wa huwal 'azeezul hakeem

4. Zaalika fadlul laahi yu'teehi many-yashaaa; wallaahu zul fadlil 'azeem

5. Masalul lazeena hum milut tawraata summa lam yahmiloonhaa kamasalil himaari yah milu asfaaraa; bi'sa masalul qawmil lazeena kaazzaboo bi aayaatil laah; wallaahu laa yahdil qawmazzaalimeen

6. Qul yaaa ayyuhal lazeena haadoo in za'amtum annakum awliyaaa'u lilaahi min doonin naasi fatamannawul mawta in kuntum saadiqeen

7. Wa laa yatamannaw nahooo abadam bimaa qaddamat aydeehim; wallaahu 'aleemum biz zaalimeen

8. Qul innal mawtal lazee tafirroona minhu fa innahoo mulaaqeekum summa turaddoona ilaa 'Aalimil Ghaibi wash shahaadati fa yunabbi'ukum bimaa kuntum ta'maloon

9. Yaaa ayyuhal lazeena aamanoo izaa noodiya lis-Salaati miny yawmil Jumu'ati fas'aw ilaa zikril laahi wa zarul bai'; zaalikum khayrul lakum in kuntum ta'lamoon

10. Fa-izaa qudiyatis Salaatu fantashiroo fil ardi wabtaghoo min fadlil laahi wazkurul laaha kaseeral la'allakum tuflihoon

11. Wa izaa ra'aw tijaaratan aw lahwanin faddooo ilaihaa wa tarakooka qaaa'imaa; qul maa 'indal laahi khairum minal lahwi wa minat tijaarah; wallaahu khayrur raaziqeen

In the name of Allah, Most Gracious, Most Merciful.

1. Whatever is in the heavens and on earth, doth declare the Praises and Glory of Allah,- the Sovereign, the Holy One, the Exalted in Might, the Wise.

2. It is He Who has sent amongst the Unlettered a messenger from among themselves, to rehearse to them His Signs, to sanctify them, and to instruct them in Scripture and Wisdom,- although they had been, before, in manifest error;-

3. As well as (to confer all these benefits upon) others of them, who have not already joined them: And He is exalted in Might, Wise.

4. Such is the Bounty of Allah, which He bestows on whom He will: and Allah is the Lord of the highest bounty.

5. The similitude of those who were charged with the (obligations of the) Mosaic Law, but who subsequently failed in those (obligations), is that of a donkey which carries huge tomes (but understands them not). Evil is the similitude of people who falsify the Signs of Allah: and Allah guides not people who do wrong.

6. Say: "O ye that stand on Judaism! If ye think that ye are friends to Allah, to the exclusion of (other) men, then express your desire for Death, if ye are truthful!"

53

7. But never will they express their desire (for Death), because of the (deeds) their hands have sent on before them! And Allah knows well those that do wrong!

8. Say: "The Death from which ye flee will truly overtake you: then will ye be sent back to the Knower of things secret and open: and He will tell you (the truth of) the things that ye did!"

9. O ye who believe! When the call is proclaimed to prayer on Friday (the Day of Assembly), hasten earnestly to the Remembrance of Allah, and leave off business (and traffic): That is best for you if ye but knew!

10. And when the Prayer is finished, then may ye disperse through the land, and seek of the Bounty of Allah: and celebrate the Praises of Allah often (and without stint): that ye may prosper.

11. But when they see some bargain or some amusement, they disperse headlong to it, and leave thee standing. Say: "The (blessing) from the Presence of Allah is better than any amusement or bargain! and Allah is the Best to provide (for all needs)."

Surah Al-Munafiqoon

Bismillaahir   Rahmaanir   Raheem
☐

1. Izaa jaaa'akal munaafiqoona qaaloo nashhadu innaka la
   rasoolul laah; wallaahu ya'lamu innaka la rasooluhoo
   wallaahu yashhadu innal munaafiqeena lakaaziboon

2. Ittakhazoo aymaanahum junnatan fasaddoo 'an sabeelil
   laah; innahum saaa'a maa kaanoo ya'maloon

3. Zaalika bi annahum aamanoo summa kafaroo fatubi'a
   'alaa quloobihim fahum laa yafqahoon

4. Wa izaa ra aytahum tu'jibuka ajsaamuhum wa iny
   yaqooloo tasma' liqawlihim kaannahum khushubum
   musannadah; yahsaboona kulla saihatin 'alaihim; humul
   'aduwwu fahzarhum; qaatalahumul laahu annaa
   yu'fakoon

5. Wa izaa qeela lahum ta'aalaw yastaghfir lakum rasoolul
   laahi lawwaw ru'oo sahum wa ra aytahum yasuddoona
   wa hum mustakbiroon

6. Sawaaa'un 'alaihim as taghfarta lahum am lam tastaghfir
   lahum lany yaghfiral laahu lahum; innal laaha laa yahdil
   qawmal faasiqeen

7. Humul lazeena yaqooloona laa tunfiqoo 'alaa man inda
   Rasoolil laahi hatta yanfaddoo; wa lillaahi khazaaa' inus
   samaawaati wal ardi wa laakinnal munaafiqeena la
   yafqahoon

8. Yaqooloona la'ir raja'naaa ilal madeenati la yukhrijanal
   a'azzu minhal azall; wa lillaahil 'izzatu wa li Rasoolihee

wa lilmu'mineena wa laakinnal munaafiqeena laa ya'lamoon

9. Yaaa ayyuhal lazeena aamanoo la tulhikum amwaalukum wa laa awlaadukum 'anzikril laah; wa mai-yaf'al zaalika fa-ulaaa'ika humul khaasiroon

10. Wa anifqoo mim maa razaqnaakum min qabli any-ya'tiya ahadakumul mawtu fa yaqoola rabbi law laaa akhkhartaneee ilaaa ajalin qareebin fa assaddaqa wa akum minassaaliheen

11. Wa lany yu 'akhkhiral laahu nafsan izaa jaaa'a ajaluhaa; wallaahu khabeerum bimaa ta'maloon

In the name of Allah, Most Gracious, Most Merciful.

1. When the Hypocrites come to thee, they say, "We bear witness that thou art indeed the Messenger of Allah." Yea, Allah knoweth that thou art indeed His Messenger, and Allah beareth witness that the Hypocrites are indeed liars.

2. They have made their oaths a screen (for their misdeeds): thus they obstruct (men) from the Path of Allah: truly evil are their deeds.

3. That is because they believed, then they rejected Faith: So a seal was set on their hearts: therefore they understand not.

4. When thou lookest at them, their exteriors please thee; and when they speak, thou listenest to their words. They are as (worthless as hollow) pieces of timber propped up, (unable to stand on their own). They think that every cry is against them. They are the enemies; so beware of them. The curse of Allah be on them! How are they deluded (away from the Truth)!

57

5. And when it is said to them, "Come, the Messenger of Allah will pray for your forgiveness", they turn aside their heads, and thou wouldst see them turning away their faces in arrogance.

6. It is equal to them whether thou pray for their forgiveness or not. Allah will not forgive them. Truly Allah guides not rebellious transgressors.

7. They are the ones who say, "Spend nothing on those who are with Allah's Messenger, to the end that they may disperse (and quit Medina)." But to Allah belong the treasures of the heavens and the earth; but the Hypocrites understand not.

8. They say, "If we return to Medina, surely the more honourable (element) will expel therefrom the meaner." But honour belongs to Allah and His Messenger, and to the Believers; but the Hypocrites know not.

9. O ye who believe! Let not your riches or your children divert you from the remembrance of Allah. If any act thus, the loss is their own.

10. And spend something (in charity) out of the substance which We have bestowed on you, before Death should come to any of you and he should say, "O my Lord! why didst Thou not give me respite for a little while? I should then have given (largely) in charity, and I should have been one of the doers of good".

11. But to no soul will Allah grant respite when the time appointed (for it) has come; and Allah is well acquainted with (all) that ye do.

Surah At-Talaq

Bismillaahir Rahmaanir Raheem

1. Yaaa ayyuhan nabiyyu izaa tallaqtummun nisaaa'a fatalliqoohunna li'iddatihinna ahsul'iddata wattaqul laaha rabbakum; laa tukhri joohunna mim bu-yootihinna wa laa yakhrujna illaaa any ya'teema bifaahishatim mubaiyinah; wa tilka hudoodul laah; wa many yata'adda hudoodal laahi faqad zalama nafsah; laa tadree la'allal laaha yuhdisu ba'dazaalika amraa

2. Fa izaa balaghna ajalahunna fa amsikoohunna bima'roofin aw faariqoohunna bima'roofinw wa ashhidoo zawai 'adlim minkum wa aqeemush shahaadata lillaah; zaalikum yoo'azu bihee man kaana yu'minu billaahi wal yawmil aakhir; wa many yattaqil laaha yaj'al lahoo makhrajaa

3. Wa yarzuqhu min haisu laa yahtasib; wa many yatawakkal 'alal laahi fahuwa husbuh; innal laaha baalighu amrih; qad ja'alal laahu likulli shai'in qadraa

4. Wallaaa'ee ya'isna minal maheedi min nisaaa 'ikum inir tabtum fa'iddatuhunna salaasatu ashhurinw wallaaa'ee lam yahidn; wa ulaatul ahmaali ajaluhunna any yada'na hamlahun; wa many yattaqil laaha yaj'al lahoo min amrihee yusraa

5. Zaalika amrul laahi anzalahoo ilaikum; wa many yattaqil laaha yukaffir 'anhu saiyi aatihee wa yu'zim lahoo ajraa

6. Askinoohunna min haisu sakantum minw wujdikum wa laa tudaaarroohunna litudaiyiqoo 'alaihinn; wa in kunna ulaati hamlin fa anfiqoo 'alaihinna hattaa yada'na hamlahunn; fain arda'na lakum fa aatoo hunna

ujoorahunn; wa'tamiroo bainakum bima'roofinw wa in
ta'aasartum fasaturdi'u lahooo ukhraa

7. Liyunfiq zoo sa'atim min sa'atih; wa man qudira 'alaihi
   rizquhoo falyunfiq mimmaaa aataahul laah; laa
   yukalliful laahu nafsan illaa maaa aataahaa; sa yaj'alul
   laahu ba'da'usriny yusraa

8. Wa ka ayyim min qaryatin 'atat 'an amri Rabbihaa wa
   Rusulihee fahaasabnaahaa hisaaban shadeedanw wa
   'azzabnaahaa 'azaaban nukraa

9. Fazaaqat wabbala amrihaa wa kaana 'aaqibatu amrihaa
   khusraa

10. A'addal laahu lahum 'azaaban shadeedan fattaqul laaha
    yaaa ulil albaab, allazeena aammanoo; qad anzalal laahu
    ilaikum zikraa

11. Rasoolany yatloo 'alaikum aayaatil laahi mubaiyinaatil
    liyukhrijal lazeena aamanoo wa 'amilus saalihaati minaz
    zulumaati ilan noor; wa many yu'min billaahi wa ya'mal
    saalihany yudkhilhu jannaatin tajree min tahtihal
    anhaaru khaalideena feehaa abadaa qad ahsanal laahu
    lahoo rizqaa

12. Allaahul lazee khalaq Sab'a Samaawaatinw wa minal
    ardi mislahunna yatanazzalul amru bainahunna
    lita'lamooo annal laaha 'alaa kulli shai'in Qadeerunw wa
    annal laaha qad ahaata bikulli shai'in 'ilmaa

In the name of Allah, Most Gracious, Most Merciful.

1. O Prophet! When ye do divorce women, divorce them at
   their prescribed periods, and count (accurately), their
   prescribed periods: And fear Allah your Lord: and turn
   them not out of their houses, nor shall they (themselves)
   leave, except in case they are guilty of some open
   lewdness, those are limits set by Allah: and any who
   transgresses the limits of Allah, does verily wrong his

61

(own) soul: thou knowest not if perchance Allah will bring about thereafter some new situation.

2. Thus when they fulfil their term appointed, either take them back on equitable terms or part with them on equitable terms; and take for witness two persons from among you, endued with justice, and establish the evidence (as) before Allah. Such is the admonition given to him who believes in Allah and the Last Day. And for those who fear Allah, He (ever) prepares a way out,

3. And He provides for him from (sources) he never could imagine. And if any one puts his trust in Allah, sufficient is (Allah) for him. For Allah will surely accomplish his purpose: verily, for all things has Allah appointed a due proportion.

4. Such of your women as have passed the age of monthly courses, for them the prescribed period, if ye have any doubts, is three months, and for those who have no courses (it is the same): for those who carry (life within their wombs), their period is until they deliver their burdens: and for those who fear Allah, He will make their path easy.

5. That is the Command of Allah, which He has sent down to you: and if any one fears Allah, He will remove his ills, from him, and will enlarge his reward.

6. Let the women live (in 'iddat) in the same style as ye live, according to your means: Annoy them not, so as to restrict them. And if they carry (life in their wombs), then spend (your substance) on them until they deliver their burden: and if they suckle your (offspring), give them their recompense: and take mutual counsel together, according to what is just and reasonable. And if ye find yourselves in difficulties, let another woman suckle (the child) on the (father's) behalf.

7. Let the man of means spend according to his means: and the man whose resources are restricted, let him spend according to what Allah has given him. Allah puts no burden on any person beyond what He has given him. After a difficulty, Allah will soon grant relief.

8. How many populations that insolently opposed the Command of their Lord and of His messengers, did We not then call to account,- to severe account?- and We imposed on them an exemplary Punishment.

9. Then did they taste the evil result of their conduct, and the End of their conduct was Perdition.

10. Allah has prepared for them a severe Punishment (in the Hereafter). Therefore fear Allah, O ye men of understanding - who have believed!- for Allah hath indeed sent down to you a Message,-

11. An Messenger, who rehearses to you the Signs of Allah containing clear explanations, that he may lead forth those who believe and do righteous deeds from the depths of Darkness into Light. And those who believe in Allah and work righteousness, He will admit to Gardens beneath which Rivers flow, to dwell therein for ever: Allah has indeed granted for them a most excellent Provision.

12. Allah is He Who created seven Firmaments and of the earth a similar number. Through the midst of them (all) descends His Command: that ye may know that Allah has power over all things, and that Allah comprehends, all things in (His) Knowledge

Surah At-Tahrim

Bismillaahir Rahmaanir Raheem

1. Yaaa ayyuhan nabiyyu lima tuharrimu maaa ahallal laahu laka tabtaghee mardaata azwaajik; wallaahu ghafoorur raheem

2. Qad faradal laahu lakum tahillata aymaanikum; wallaahu mawlaakum wa huwal 'aleemul hakeem

3. Wa iz asarran nabiyyu ilaa ba'di azwaajihee hadeesan falammaa nabba at bihee wa azharahul laahu 'alaihi 'arrafa ba'dahoo wa a'rada 'am ba'din falammaa nabba ahaa bihee qaalat man amba aka haaza qaala nabba aniyal 'aleemul khabeer

4. In tatoobaaa ilal laahi faqad saghat quloobukumaa wa in tazaaharaa 'alaihi fa innal laaha huwa mawlaahu wa jibreelu wa saalihul mu'mineen; wal malaaa'ikatu ba'dazaalika zaheer

5. 'Asaa rabbuhooo in tallaqakunna anyyubdilahooo azwaajan khairam minkunna muslimaatim mu'minaatin qaanitaatin taaa'ibaatin 'aabidaatin saaa'ihaatin saiyibaatinw wa abkaaraa

6. Yaaa ayyuhal lazeena aamanoo qooo anfusakum wa ahleekum naaranw waqooduhan naasu wal hijaaratu 'alaihaa malaaa'ikatun ghilaazun shidaadul laa ya'soonal laaha maa amarahum wa yaf'aloona maa yu'maroon

7. Yaaa ayyuhal lazeena kafaroo la ta'tazirul yawma innamaa tujzawna maa kuntum ta'maloon

8. Yaaa ayyuhal lazeena aamanoo toobooo ilal laahi tawbatan nasoohan 'asaa rabbukum any-yukaffira 'ankum sayyi aatikum wa yudkhilakum jannaatin tajree

min tahtihal anhaaru yawma laa yukhzil laahun nabiyya wallazeena aamanoo ma'ahoo nooruhum yas'aa baina aydeehim wa bi aymaanihim yaqooloona rabbanaaa atmim lanaa nooranaa waghfir lana innaka 'alaa kulli shai'in qadeer

9. Yaaa ayyuhan nabiyyu jaahidil kuffaara walmunaa-fiqeena waghluz 'alaihim; wa ma'waahum jahannamu wa bi'sal maser

10. Darabal laahu masalal lillazeena kafarum ra ata Noohinw wamra ata Loot, kaanataa tahta 'abdaini min 'ibaadinaa saalihaini fakhaanataahumaa falam yughniyaa 'anhumaa minal laahi shai anw-wa qeelad khulan naara ma'ad Daakhileen

11. Wa darabal laahu masalal lil lezeena aamanumra ata Fir'awn; iz qaalat rab bibni lee 'indaka baitan fil jannati wa najjinee min Fir'awna wa 'amalihee wa najjinee minal qawmiz zaalimeen

12. Wa Maryamab nata 'Imraanal lateee ahsanat farjahaa fanafakhnaa feehee mir roohinaa wa saddaqat bi kalimaati Rabhihaa wa Kutubihee wakaanati minal qaaniteen

In the name of Allah, Most Gracious, Most Merciful.

1. O Prophet! Why holdest thou to be forbidden that which Allah has made lawful to thee? Thou seekest to please thy consorts. But Allah is Oft-Forgiving, Most Merciful.

2. Allah has already ordained for you, (O men), the dissolution of your oaths (in some cases): and Allah is your Protector, and He is full of Knowledge and Wisdom.

3. When the Prophet disclosed a matter in confidence to one of his consorts, and she then divulged it (to another), and Allah made it known to him, he confirmed part

thereof and repudiated a part. Then when he told her thereof, she said, "Who told thee this? "He said, "He told me Who knows and is well-acquainted (with all things)."

4. If ye two turn in repentance to Him, your hearts are indeed so inclined; But if ye back up each other against him, truly Allah is his Protector, and Gabriel, and (every) righteous one among those who believe,- and furthermore, the angels - will back (him) up.

5. It may be, if he divorced you (all), that Allah will give him in exchange consorts better than you,- who submit (their wills), who believe, who are devout, who turn to Allah in repentance, who worship (in humility), who travel (for Faith) and fast,- previously married or virgins.

6. O ye who believe! save yourselves and your families from a Fire whose fuel is Men and Stones, over which are (appointed) angels stern (and) severe, who flinch not (from executing) the Commands they receive from Allah, but do (precisely) what they are commanded.

7. (They will say), "O ye Unbelievers! Make no excuses this Day! Ye are being but requited for all that ye did!"

8. O ye who believe! Turn to Allah with sincere repentance: In the hope that your Lord will remove from you your ills and admit you to Gardens beneath which Rivers flow,- the Day that Allah will not permit to be humiliated the Prophet and those who believe with him. Their Light will run forward before them and by their right hands, while they say, "Our Lord! Perfect our Light for us, and grant us Forgiveness: for Thou hast power over all things."

9. O Prophet! Strive hard against the Unbelievers and the Hypocrites, and be firm against them. Their abode is Hell,- an evil refuge (indeed).

10. Allah sets forth, for an example to the Unbelievers, the wife of Noah and the wife of Lut: they were (respectively) under two of our righteous servants, but they were false to their (husbands), and they profited nothing before Allah on their account, but were told: "Enter ye the Fire along with (others) that enter!"

11. And Allah sets forth, as an example to those who believe the wife of Pharaoh: Behold she said: "O my Lord! Build for me, in nearness to Thee, a mansion in the Garden, and save me from Pharaoh and his doings, and save me from those that do wrong";

12. And Mary the daughter of 'Imran, who guarded her chastity; and We breathed into (her body) of Our spirit; and she testified to the truth of the words of her Lord and of His Revelations, and was one of the devout (servants).

Surah Al-Ikhlas

Bismillaahir Rahmaanir Raheem

1. Qul huwal laahu ahad
2. Allah hus-samad
3. Lam yalid wa lam yoolad
4. Wa lam yakul-lahu kufuwan ahad

In the name of Allah, Most Gracious, Most Merciful.

1. Say: He is Allah, the One and Only;
2. Allah, the Eternal, Absolute;
3. He begetteth not, nor is He begotten;
4. And there is none like unto Him.

Surah As-Saff

Bismillaahir Rahmaanir Raheem

1. Sabbaha lillaahi maa fisamaawaati wa maa fil ardi wa huwal 'Azeezul Hakeem

2. Yaa ayyuhal lazeena aamanoo lima taqooloona maa laa taf'aloon

3. Kabura maqtan 'indal laahi an taqooloo maa laa taf'aloon

4. Innal laaha yuhibbul lazeena yuqaatiloona fee sabeelihee saffan ka annahum bunyaanum marsoos

5. Wa iz qaala Moosa liqawmihee yaa qawmi lima tu'zoonanee wa qat ta'lamoona annee Rasoolul laahi ilaikum falammaa zaaghoo azaaghal laahu quloobahum; wallaahu laa yahdil qawmal faasiqeen

6. Wa iz qaala 'Eesab-nu-Mayama yaa Banee Israaa'eela innee Rasoolul laahi ilaikum musaddiqal limaa baina yadayya minat Tawraati wa mubashshiram bi Rasooliny yaatee mim ba'dis muhooo Ahmad; falammaa jaaa'ahum bil baiyinaati qaaloo haazaa sihrum mubeen

7. Wa man azlamu mimma nif taraa 'alal laahil kaziba wa huwa yad'aaa ilal Islaam; wallaahu laa yahdil qawmaz zaalimeen

8. Yureedoona liyutfi'oo nooral laahi bi afwaahihim wallaahu mutimmu noorihee wa law karihal kaafiroon

9. Huwal lazee arsala Rasoolahoo bilhudaa wa deenil haqqi liyuzhirahoo 'alad deeni kullihee wa law karihal mushrikoon

10. Yaaa ayyuhal lazeena aamanoo hal adullukum 'alaa tijaaratin tunjeekum min 'azaabin aleem

11. Tu'minoona billaahi wa Rasoolihee wa tujaahidoona fee sabeelil laahi bi amwaalikum wa anfusikum; zaalikum khairul lakum in kuntum ta'lamoon

12. Yaghfir lakum zunoobakum wa yudkhilkum Jannaatin tajree min tahtihal anhaaru wa masaakina taiyibatan fee Jannaati 'Adn; zaalikal fawzul 'Azeem

13. Wa ukhraa tuhibboonahaa nasrum minal laahi wa fat hun qareeb; wa bashshiril mu 'mineen

14. Yaaa ayyuhal lazeena aamanoo koonooo ansaaral laahi kamaa qaala 'Eesab-nu-Maryama lil Hawaariyyeena man ansaareee ilal laah; qaalal Hawaariyyoona nahnu ansaa rul laahi fa aamanat taaa'ifatum mim Bannee Israaa'eela wa kafarat taaa'ifatun fa ayyadnal lazeena aamanoo 'alaa 'aduwwihim fa asbahoo zaahireen

In the name of Allah, Most Gracious, Most Merciful.

1. Whatever is in the heavens and on earth, let it declare the Praises and Glory of Allah: for He is the Exalted in Might, the Wise.

2. O ye who believe! Why say ye that which ye do not?

3. Grievously odious is it in the sight of Allah that ye say that which ye do not.

4. Truly Allah loves those who fight in His Cause in battle array, as if they were a solid cemented structure.

5. And remember, Moses said to his people: "O my people! why do ye vex and insult me, though ye know that I am the messenger of Allah (sent) to you?" Then when they went wrong, Allah let their hearts go wrong. For Allah guides not those who are rebellious transgressors.

71

6. And remember, Jesus, the son of Mary, said: "O Children of Israel! I am the messenger of Allah (sent) to you, confirming the Law (which came) before me, and giving Glad Tidings of a Messenger to come after me, whose name shall be Ahmad." But when he came to them with Clear Signs, they said, "this is evident sorcery!"

7. Who doth greater wrong than one who invents falsehood against Allah, even as he is being invited to Islam? And Allah guides not those who do wrong.

8. Their intention is to extinguish Allah's Light (by blowing) with their mouths: But Allah will complete (the revelation of) His Light, even though the Unbelievers may detest (it).

9. It is He Who has sent His Messenger with Guidance and the Religion of Truth, that he may proclaim it over all religion, even though the Pagans may detest (it).

10. O ye who believe! Shall I lead you to a bargain that will save you from a grievous Penalty?-

11. That ye believe in Allah and His Messenger, and that ye strive (your utmost) in the Cause of Allah, with your property and your persons: That will be best for you, if ye but knew!

12. He will forgive you your sins, and admit you to Gardens beneath which Rivers flow, and to beautiful mansions in Gardens of Eternity: that is indeed the Supreme Achievement.

13. And another (favour will He bestow,) which ye do love,- help from Allah and a speedy victory. So give the Glad Tidings to the Believers.

14. O ye who believe! Be ye helpers of Allah: As said Jesus the son of Mary to the Disciples, "Who will be my helpers to (the work of) Allah?" Said the disciples, "We are Allah's helpers!" then a portion of the Children of Israel believed, and a portion disbelieved: But We gave power to those who believed, against their enemies, and they became the ones that prevailed.

Surah Al-Hujuraat

Bismillaahir Rahmaanir Raheem

1. Yaa ayyuhal lazeena aamanoo la tuqaddimoo baina yada yil laahi wa Rasoolihee wattaqul laah; innal laaha samee'un 'Aleem

2. Yaa ayyuhal lazeena aamanoo laa tarfa'ooo aswaatakum fawqa sawtin Nabiyi wa laa tajharoo lahoo bilqawli kajahri ba'dikum liba 'din an tahbata a 'maalukum wa antum laa tash'uroon

3. Innal lazeena yaghud doona aswaatahum 'inda Rasoolil laahi ulaaa'ikal lazeenam tah anal laahu quloobahum littaqwaa; lahum maghfiratunw waajrun 'azeem

4. Innal lazeena yunaadoo naka minw waraaa'il hujuraati aksaruhum laa ya'qiloon

5. Wa law annahum sabaroo hatta takhruja ilaihim lakaana khairal lahum; wallaahu Ghafoorur Raheem

6. Yaaa ayyuhal lazeena aamanoo in jaaa'akum faasqum binaba in fatabaiyanooo an tuseeboo qawmam bijahalatin fatusbihoo 'alaa maa fa'altum naadimeen

7. Wa'lamooo anna feekum Rasoolal laah; law yutee'ukum fee kaseerim minal amrila'anittum wa laakinnal laaha habbaba ilaikumul eemaana wa zaiyanahoo fee quloobikum wa karraha ilaikumul kufra walfusooqa wal'isyaan; ulaaaika humur raashidoon

8. Fadlam minal laahi wa ni'mah; wallaahu 'Aleemun Hakeem

9. Wa in taaa'ifataani minal mu'mineena naqtataloo fa aslihoo bainahumaa; fa-im baghat ihdaahumaa 'alal ukhraa faqaatilul latee tabghee hattaa tafeee'a ilaaa amril

74

laah; fa-in faaa'at fa aslihoo bainahumaa bil'adli wa aqsitoo, innal laaha yuhibbul muqsiteen

10. Innamal mu'minoona ikhwatun fa aslihoo baina akhawaykum wattaqul laaha la'allakum tuhamoon

11. Yaaa ayyuhal lazeena aamanoo laa yaskhar qawmum min qawmin 'asaaa anyyakoonoo khairam minhum wa laa nisaaa'um min nisaaa'in 'Asaaa ay yakunna khairam minhunna wa laa talmizooo anfusakum wa laa tanaabazoo bil alqaab; bi'sal ismul fusooqu ba'dal eemaan; wa mal-lam yatub fa-ulaaa'ika humuz zaalimoon

12. Yaaa ayyuhal lazeena aamanuj taniboo kaseeram minaz zanni inna ba'daz zanniismunw wa laa tajassasoo wa la yaghtab ba'dukum ba'daa; a yuhibbu ahadukum any yaakula lahma akheehi maitan fakarih tumooh; wattaqul laa; innal laaha tawwaabur Raheem

13. Yaaa ayyuhan naasu innaa khalaqnaakum min zakarinw wa unsaa wa ja'alnaakum shu'oobanw wa qabaaa'ila lita'arafoo inna akramakum 'indal laahi atqaakum innal laaha 'Aleemun khabeer

14. Qaalatil-A 'raabu aamannaa qul lam tu'minoo wa laakin qoolooo aslamnaa wa lamma yadkhulil eemaanu fee quloobikum wa in tutee'ul laaha wa Rasoolahoo laa yalitkum min a'maalikum shai'aa; innal laaha Ghafoorur Raheem

15. Innamal muu'minoonal lazeena aamanoo billaahi wa Rasoolihee summa lam yartaaboo wa jaahadoo biamwaalihim wa anfusihim fee sabeelil laah; ulaaaika humus saadiqoon

16. Qul atu'allimoonal laaha bideenikum wallaahu ya'lamu maa fis samaawaati wa maa fil ard; wallaahu bikulli shai'in 'Aleem

17. Yamunnoona 'alaika an aslamoo qul laa tamunnoo 'alaiya Islaamakum balillaahu yamunnu 'alaikum an hadaakum lil eemaani in kuntum saadiqeen

18. Innal laaha ya'lamu ghaibas samaawaati wal ard; wallaahu baseerum bimaa ta'maloon

In the name of Allah, Most Gracious, Most Merciful.

1. O Ye who believe! Put not yourselves forward before Allah and His Messenger; but fear Allah: for Allah is He Who hears and knows all things.

2. O ye who believe! Raise not your voices above the voice of the Prophet, nor speak aloud to him in talk, as ye may speak aloud to one another, lest your deeds become vain and ye perceive not.

3. Those that lower their voices in the presence of Allah's Messenger,- their hearts has Allah tested for piety: for them is Forgiveness and a great Reward.

4. Those who shout out to thee from without the inner apartments - most of them lack understanding.

5. If only they had patience until thou couldst come out to them, it would be best for them: but Allah is Oft-Forgiving, Most Merciful.

6. O ye who believe! If a wicked person comes to you with any news, ascertain the truth, lest ye harm people unwittingly, and afterwards become full of repentance for what ye have done.

7. And know that among you is Allah's Messenger: were he, in many matters, to follow your (wishes), ye would certainly fall into misfortune: But Allah has endeared the Faith to you, and has made it beautiful in your hearts, and He has made hateful to you Unbelief, wickedness,

76

and rebellion: such indeed are those who walk in righteousness;-

8. A Grace and Favour from Allah; and Allah is full of Knowledge and Wisdom.

9. If two parties among the Believers fall into a quarrel, make ye peace between them: but if one of them transgresses beyond bounds against the other, then fight ye (all) against the one that transgresses until it complies with the command of Allah; but if it complies, then make peace between them with justice, and be fair: for Allah loves those who are fair (and just).

10. The Believers are but a single Brotherhood: So make peace and reconciliation between your two (contending) brothers; and fear Allah, that ye may receive Mercy.

11. O ye who believe! Let not some men among you laugh at others: It may be that the (latter) are better than the (former): Nor let some women laugh at others: It may be that the (latter are better than the (former): Nor defame nor be sarcastic to each other, nor call each other by (offensive) nicknames: Ill-seeming is a name connoting wickedness, (to be used of one) after he has believed: And those who do not desist are (indeed) doing wrong.

12. O ye who believe! Avoid suspicion as much (as possible): for suspicion in some cases is a sin: And spy not on each other behind their backs. Would any of you like to eat the flesh of his dead brother? Nay, ye would abhor it...But fear Allah: For Allah is Oft-Returning, Most Merciful.

13. O mankind! We created you from a single (pair) of a male and a female, and made you into nations and tribes, that ye may know each other (not that ye may despise (each other). Verily the most honoured of you in the sight of Allah is (he who is) the most righteous of you.

And Allah has full knowledge and is well acquainted (with all things).

14. The desert Arabs say, "We believe." Say, "Ye have no faith; but ye (only)say, 'We have submitted our wills to Allah,' For not yet has Faith entered your hearts. But if ye obey Allah and His Messenger, He will not belittle aught of your deeds: for Allah is Oft-Forgiving, Most Merciful."

15. Only those are Believers who have believed in Allah and His Messenger, and have never since doubted, but have striven with their belongings and their persons in the Cause of Allah: Such are the sincere ones.

16. Say: "What! Will ye instruct Allah about your religion? But Allah knows all that is in the heavens and on earth: He has full knowledge of all things.

17. They impress on thee as a favour that they have embraced Islam. Say, "Count not your Islam as a favour upon me: Nay, Allah has conferred a favour upon you that He has guided you to the faith, if ye be true and sincere.

18. "Verily Allah knows the secrets of the heavens and the earth: and Allah Sees well all that ye do."

Surah At-Taghabun

Bismillaahir Rahmaanir Raheem

1. Yusabbihu lillaahi maa fis samaawaati wa maa fil ardi lahul mulku wa lahul hamd, wa Huwa 'alaa kulli shai 'in Qadeer

2. Huwal lazee khalaqakum faminkum kaafirunw wa min kum mu'min ; wallaahu bimaa ta'maloona Baseer

3. Khalaqas samaawaati wal arda bilhaqqi wa sawwarakum fa ahsana suwarakum wa ilaihil maser

4. Ya'lamu maa fis samaawaati wal ardi wa ya'lamu maa tusirroona wa maa tu'linoon; wallaahu 'Aleemum bizaatis sudoor

5. Alam ya'tikum naba'ul lazeena kafaroo min qablu fazaaqoo wabaala amrihim wa lahum 'azaabun aleem

6. Zaalika bi annahoo kaanat ta'teehim Rusuluhum bilbaiyinaati faqaaloo a basharuny yahdoonanaa fakafaroo wa tawallaw; wastaghnal laah; wallaahu ghaniyyun hameed

7. Za'amal lazeena kafarooo al-lany yub'asoo; qul balaa wa rabbee latub'asunna summa latunabba'unna bimaa 'amiltum; wa zaalika 'alal laahi yaseer

8. Fa-aaminoo billaahi wa rasoolihee wannooril lazeee anzalnaa; wallaahu bima ta'maloona khabeer

9. Yawma yajma'ukum li yawmil jam'i zaalika yawmut taghaabun; wa many-yumim billaahi wa ya'mal saalihany yukaffir 'anhu sayyi aatihee wa yudkhilhu jannaatin tajree min tahtihal anhaaru khaalideena feehaaa abadaa; zaalikal fawzul 'azeem

10. Wallazeena kafaroo wa kazzaboo bi aayaaatinaaa ulaaa'ika ashaabun naari khaalideena feehaa wa bi'sal maser

11. Maaa asaaba mim musee batin illaa bi-iznil laah; wa many yu'mim billaahi yahdi qalbah; wallaahu bikulli shai'in Aleem

12. Wa atee'ul laaha wa atee'ur Rasool; fa in tawallaitum fa innamaa 'alaa Rasoolinal balaaghul mubeen

13. Allaahu laaa ilaaha illaa Hoo; wa 'alal laahi falyata wakkalil mu'minoon

14. Yaaa ayyuhal lazeena aamanooo inna min azwaaji kum wa awlaadikum 'aduwwal lakum fahzaroohum; wa in ta'foo wa tasfahoo wa taghfiroo fa innal laaha ghafoorur Raheem

15. Innamaa amwaalukum wa awlaadukum fitnah; wallaahu 'indahooo ajrun 'azeem

16. Fattaqul laaha mastata'tum wasma'oo wa atee'oo wa anfiqoo khairal li anfusikum; wa many-yooqa shuh ha nafsihee fa-ulaaa'ika humul muflihoon

17. In tuqridul laaha qardan hasanany yudaaifhu lakum wa yaghfir lakum; wallaahu Shakoorun Haleem

18. 'Aalimul-Ghaibi wash-shahaadatil 'Azeezul Hakeem

In the name of Allah, Most Gracious, Most Merciful.

1. Whatever is in the heavens and on earth, doth declare the Praises and Glory of Allah: to Him belongs dominion, and to Him belongs praise: and He has power over all things.

2. It is He Who has created you; and of you are some that are Unbelievers, and some that are Believers: and Allah sees well all that ye do.

3. He has created the heavens and the earth in just proportions, and has given you shape, and made your shapes beautiful: and to Him is the final Goal.

4. He knows what is in the heavens and on earth; and He knows what ye conceal and what ye reveal: yea, Allah knows well the (secrets) of (all) hearts.

5. Has not the story reached you, of those who rejected Faith aforetime? So they tasted the evil result of their conduct; and they had a grievous Penalty.

6. That was because there came to them messengers with Clear Signs, but they said: "Shall (mere) human beings direct us?" So they rejected (the Message) and turned away. But Allah can do without (them): and Allah is free of all needs, worthy of all praise.

7. The Unbelievers think that they will not be raised up (for Judgment). Say: "Yea, By my Lord, Ye shall surely be raised up: then shall ye be told (the truth) of all that ye did. And that is easy for Allah."

8. Believe, therefore, in Allah and His Messenger, and in the Light which we have sent down. And Allah is well acquainted with all that ye do.

9. The Day that He assembles you (all) for a Day of Assembly,- that will be a Day of mutual loss and gain (among you), and those who believe in Allah and work righteousness,- He will remove from them their ills, and He will admit them to Gardens beneath which Rivers flow, to dwell therein for ever: that will be the Supreme Achievement.

10. But those who reject Faith and treat Our Signs as falsehoods, they will be Companions of the Fire, to dwell therein for aye: and evil is that Goal.

11. No kind of calamity can occur, except by the leave of Allah: and if any one believes in Allah, (Allah) guides his heart (aright): for Allah knows all things.

12. So obey Allah, and obey His Messenger: but if ye turn back, the duty of Our Messenger is but to proclaim (the Message) clearly and openly.

13. Allah! There is no god but He: and on Allah, therefore, let the Believers put their trust.

14. O ye who believe! Truly, among your wives and your children are (some that are) enemies to yourselves: so beware of them! But if ye forgive and overlook, and cover up (their faults), verily Allah is Oft-Forgiving, Most Merciful.

15. Your riches and your children may be but a trial: but in the Presence of Allah, is the highest, Reward.

16. So fear Allah as much as ye can; listen and obey and spend in charity for the benefit of your own soul and those saved from the covetousness of their own souls,- they are the ones that achieve prosperity.

17. If ye loan to Allah, a beautiful loan, He will double it to your (credit), and He will grant you Forgiveness: for Allah is most Ready to appreciate (service), Most Forbearing,-

18. Knower of what is open, Exalted in Might, Full of Wisdom.

Ayatul Kursi

Bismillaahir Rahmaanir Raheem
Allahu laaa ilaaha illaa huwal haiyul qai-yoom; laa taakhuzuhoo sinatunw wa laa nawm; lahoo maa fissamaawaati wa maa fil ard; man zallazee yashfa'u indahooo illaa be iznih; ya'lamu maa baina aideehim wa maa khalfahum; wa laa yuheetoona beshai 'immin 'ilmihee illa be maa shaaaa; wasi'a kursiyyuhus samaa waati wal arda wa la ya'ooduho hifzuhumaa; wa huwal aliyyul 'azeem.

Allah! There is no god but He - the Living, the Self-subsisting, Eternal. No slumber can seize Him nor Sleep. His are all things in the heavens and on earth. Who is there can intercede in His presence except as he permitteth? He knoweth what (appeareth to His creatures As) Before or After or Behind them. Nor shall they compass aught of His knowledge except as He willeth. His throne doth extend over the heavens and on earth, and He feeleth no fatigue in guarding and preserving them, For He is the Most High, the Supreme (in glory)."

About Ayatul Kursi

The Throne Verse (Arabic: اَيَةُ الْكُرْسِي, 'āyat al-kursī) is the 255th verse of the 2nd surah of the Quran, Al-Baqarah. The verse speaks about how nothing and nobody is regarded to be comparable to Allah.

This is one of the best-known verses of the Quran and is widely memorised and displayed in the Islamic world. It is often recited to ward off evil spirits

Ayat al-Kursi is regarded as one of the most powerful ayahs in the Quran because when it is recited, the greatness of God is believed to be confirmed. The person who recites this ayah morning and evening will be under protection of God from the evil of the jinn and the shayatin (demons); this is also known as the daily adkhar. It is used in exorcism, to cure and protect from jinn and shayatin. Because the Throne Verse is believed to grant spiritual or physical protection, it is often recited by Muslims before setting out on a journey and before going to sleep.

Narrated Abu Huraira: Allah's Messenger (ﷺ) deputed me to keep Sadaqat (al-Fitr) of Ramadan. A comer came and started taking handfuls of the foodstuff (of the Sadaqa) (stealthily). I took hold of him and said, "By Allah, I will take you to Allah's Messenger (ﷺ) ." He said, "I am needy and have many dependents, and I am in great need." I released him, and in the morning Allah's Messenger (ﷺ) asked me, "What did your prisoner do yesterday?" I said, "O Allah's Messenger (ﷺ!) The person complained of being needy and of having many dependents, so, I pitied him and let him go." Allah's Messenger (ﷺ) said, "Indeed, he told you a lie and he will be coming again." I believed that he would show up again as Allah's Messenger (ﷺ) had told me that he would return. So, I waited for him watchfully. When he (showed up and) started stealing handfuls of foodstuff, I caught hold of him again and said, "I will definitely take you to Allah's Messenger (ﷺ.) He said, "Leave me, for I am very needy and have many dependents. I promise I will not come back again." I pitied him and let him go. In the morning Allah's Messenger (ﷺ) asked me, "What did your prisoner do." I replied, "O Allah's Messenger (ﷺ)! He complained of his great need and of too many dependents, so I took pity on him and set him free." Allah's Apostle said, "Verily, he told you a lie and he will return." I waited for him attentively for the third time, and when he (came and) started stealing handfuls of the foodstuff, I caught hold of him and said, "I will surely take you to Allah's Messenger (ﷺ) as it is the third time you promise not to return, yet you break your promise and come." He said, "(Forgive me and) I will teach you some words with which Allah will benefit you." I asked, "What are they?" He replied, "Whenever you go to bed, recite "Ayat-al-Kursi"-- 'Allahu la ilaha illa huwa-l-Haiy-ul Qaiyum' till you finish the whole verse. (If you do so), Allah will appoint a guard for you who will stay with you and no satan will come near you till morning. "So, I released him. In the morning, Allah's Apostle asked, "What did your prisoner do yesterday?" I replied, "He claimed that he would teach me some words by which Allah will benefit me, so I let him go." Allah's Messenger (ﷺ) asked, "What are they?" I replied, "He said to me, 'Whenever you go to bed, recite Ayat-al-Kursi from the beginning to the end ---- Allahu la ilaha illa huwa-lHaiy-ul-Qaiyum----.' He further said to me, '(If you do so), Allah will appoint a guard for you who will stay with you, and no satan will come near you till morning.' (Abu Huraira or another sub-narrator) added that they (the companions) were very keen to do good deeds. The Prophet (ﷺ) said, "He really spoke the truth, although he is an absolute liar. Do you know whom you were talking to, these three nights, O Abu

Huraira?" Abu Huraira said, "No." He said, "It was Satan."

— Sahih al-Bukhari 2311

Printed in Great Britain
by Amazon

39037288R00056